Original title:
Renewing Our Love

Copyright © 2024 Swan Charm
All rights reserved.

Author: Olivia Orav
ISBN HARDBACK: 978-9916-89-181-0
ISBN PAPERBACK: 978-9916-89-182-7
ISBN EBOOK: 978-9916-89-183-4

The Light Between Us Reborn

In shadows deep, we find our spark,
With every glance, we leave the dark.
Together we rise, like stars that gleam,
Your warmth ignites my hidden dream.

A flicker grows into a flame,
Our souls entwined, we're never the same.
In every whisper, in every sigh,
The light between us cannot die.

Tides of Affection Anew

Waves crash softly on the shore,
A rhythm we can't ignore.
With each tide, love finds its way,
A dance of hearts, come what may.

Beneath the moon, our shadows sway,
In currents strong, we choose to stay.
The ebb and flow, a sweet caress,
In tides of love, we find our rest.

Hearts Unfurling in the Dawn

Awakened by the songs of morn,
Our dreams take flight, together born.
With every ray of golden light,
Our hearts unfurl, ready for flight.

In gentle breezes, hope does soar,
A promise whispered, evermore.
In the dawn's embrace, we find our truth,
A love renewed, a treasure of youth.

Repainting Our Shared Canvas

Brushes dance on a vibrant hue,
Together we create anew.
With every stroke, our stories blend,
A masterpiece that has no end.

In shades of laughter, tears, and care,
Our canvas speaks of love laid bare.
With every color, we ignite,
Repainting life in pure delight.

Rekindling the Fireflies

In the dusk of fading light,
Whispers dance on gentle sighs,
Memories twinkle in the night,
Hope ignites as fireflies rise.

Each flicker tells a tale so sweet,
Of lovers lost and found once more,
In shadows where our hearts can meet,
We chase the glow, forever soar.

Through fields of dreams, we wander slow,
Where laughter mingles with the stars,
With every spark, our spirits grow,
Rekindled flames, erasing scars.

Threads of Yesterday

In the tapestry of time's embrace,
Old memories weave a gentle thread,
Golden moments we cannot erase,
Each stitch whispers secrets we've said.

Faded photographs, laughter's sound,
Capture the joy we used to share,
In the fabric of life, we're found,
Through every joy and every care.

The threads intertwine in colors bright,
A vibrant dance of loss and gain,
In the morning's soft, glimmering light,
We find the warmth within the pain.

Woven Anew

With hands outstretched, we plant the seeds,
In fertile soil, we sow our dreams,
Tangled paths, we follow needs,
Woven anew, our future gleams.

The loom of time spins threads of gold,
In every challenge, strength appears,
Together, brave, our hearts are bold,
We stitch our hopes through joy and tears.

Each knot a promise, every tie,
In patterns rich, we shape our fate,
As seasons pass and moments fly,
Our fabric grows, we celebrate.

The Garden of Unfaded Dreams

In a garden where the wildflowers sway,
Colors burst beneath the sun's embrace,
Every petal whispers night and day,
In this haven, dreams find their place.

Beneath the arch of a silvered moon,
Stars twinkle like seeds in the air,
In the quiet, sweet melodies croon,
Encouraging hope, with tender care.

Here, we gather memories bright,
Tending to hopes like fragile blooms,
In the heart's sanctuary of light,
We cultivate love that forever looms.

A Symphony of Soft Beginnings

Dawn breaks gently with a tender song,
Nature hums in every sweet refrain,
As the world stirs, it feels so strong,
A symphony that echoes in the rain.

With each note, new stories arise,
A dance of hope, a breath of grace,
In the chorus where the heart complies,
Life unfolds at its own pace.

Together, we embrace the dawn,
As colors blend in morning light,
In soft beginnings, we are drawn,
To a melody that feels so right.

Together Again

In the sunlight's warm embrace,
We find our hearts collide.
The laughter shared, the smiles bright,
In unity, we take our stride.

Each moment echoes in our souls,
A bond that time cannot sever.
Through trials faced and rivers crossed,
We rise above, together forever.

A Fresh Start

Beneath the dawn's gentle hue,
A canvas wide awaits anew.
With courage stitched in every seam,
We paint our hopes, we weave our dream.

The past may linger, but we soar,
With open hearts, we seek the more.
Each step we take, a brighter way,
In the fresh blooms of a new day.

Echoes of Affection

In whispered winds, your love still sings,
A melody of gentle things.
Through shadows deep, your light remains,
In echoes sweet, it softly reigns.

The memories dance like leaves in flight,
A tapestry of pure delight.
In every heartbeat, every sigh,
Your love's a force that won't say die.

Garden of Second Chances

In fertile soil, we plant our dreams,
With hope that blooms in endless beams.
Though storms may come to bend and break,
Resilience grows for love's own sake.

Each petal soft, each color bright,
A testament to past's own fight.
With every dawn, new life shall rise,
In this garden, love defies.

Embrace of New Beginnings

With open arms, we greet the light,
In every dawn, our spirits bright.
The past is but a distant shore,
We step ahead, seek something more.

Each moment holds a chance to grow,
To chase the dreams that softly flow.
In unity, we find our wings,
As life unfolds, new joy it brings.

Reflections in the Heart

In quiet moments, shadows dance,
Whispers echo, a fleeting chance.
Mirrors of choice, they softly gleam,
A world of thoughts, a secret dream.

Time passes slow, like drops of dew,
Each memory lingers, tender and true.
Fractured pieces, they bind anew,
In silence echo, the heart's debut.

Through light and dark, we find our way,
Each reflection, a soft ballet.
In depths of love, where hopes reside,
A gentle tide, in the heart, abide.

Waves of longing, pull us near,
Lost in the chorus, we shed a tear.
In every glance, a story told,
An inner warmth, a love unrolled.

Every heartbeat, a melody plays,
In the stillness, time gently sways.
With each embrace, we mend the seams,
Reflections glow, like woven dreams.

The Journey Back to You

Winding roads beneath the stars,
Memories whisper, near and far.
Each step forward, a chance to find,
The love that lingers, intertwined.

Through valleys low and mountains high,
I chase the echoes, a heartfelt sigh.
In every shadow, your light shines through,
A beacon calling, guiding me to you.

The path is long, but feet feel light,
With every heartbeat, I seek your sight.
In dreams we share, the moments bloom,
A promise kept, dispelling gloom.

With every dawn, new hope is born,
Through laughter shared, and hearts reborn.
In tender whispers, we rewrite fate,
On the journey back, no need to wait.

At the journey's end, I stand with grace,
Time pauses soft, in your embrace.
Together we'll rewrite history's view,
Forever bound, in love so true.

Mosaic of Emotions

Pieces of life, colors collide,
In a canvas bright, where dreams abide.
Fragments of laughter, sorrow and light,
Each stroke tells stories, day and night.

In every corner, a shade of care,
A patchwork woven, rich and rare.
Joy meets sorrow, together they blend,
In the heart's gallery, there lies no end.

Moments captured, like stars in the sky,
Each one a treasure, a reason why.
In silence gathered, colors we find,
A mosaic of emotions, forever entwined.

Through the chaos, a thread remains,
In every heartbeat, love sustains.
A tapestry woven with tender grace,
In the vast expanse, we find our place.

Life's hues may fade, yet still they thrive,
In every heartbeat, together we'll strive.
An artwork crafted, bold and true,
Our journey unfolds, just me and you.

A Love Reawakened

Flickers of flame, once dimmed by time,
A heartbeat whispers, love's subtle chime.
In shadows cast, a spark ignites,
Rekindled passion, the heart's delights.

Through tangled paths, we've walked alone,
In distant memories, seeds were sown.
Through trials faced, we've grown anew,
A love reawakened, fresh as the dew.

Under starlit skies, our souls align,
In gentle sighs, your hand in mine.
With every glance, the past we trace,
A lingering warmth, a sweet embrace.

In every moment, we find our way,
Remnants of laughter, forever stay.
Through storms endured, we rise and shine,
In love's embrace, forever entwined.

The journey continues, hand in hand,
In every heartbeat, a new command.
A love reawakened, pure and bright,
Together we'll bask in the soft moonlight.

New Horizons of Togetherness

In the dawn of a shared dream,
We rise as one, hand in hand.
The sky unfolds in vibrant beams,
Uniting hearts across the land.

In whispered hopes, our spirits soar,
Echoes of laughter in the air.
With every step, we seek for more,
Together, free from every care.

Through valleys low and mountains high,
Our bond, a compass guiding true.
With courage found in every sigh,
No challenge vast, we'll not pursue.

As rivers flow and seasons change,
We navigate this vast expanse.
In love, we find the sweetest range,
Together, weaving our own dance.

The stars above, our witness bright,
With every twinkle, dreams ignite.
New horizons call, we embrace the light,
Together, we'll take flight tonight.

Echoes of Our Journey

Along the path where shadows play,
Footprints linger, stories told.
Memories weave in bright array,
In echoes soft, our hearts unfold.

The laughter shared, the tears we've cried,
Moments cherished, deeply sown.
In every twist, love's glow supplied,
Together, never more alone.

Through storms we've faced and skies of blue,
Each chapter penned with threads of grace.
In every challenge, found anew,
Our journey marked in time and space.

As seasons change, we'll walk anew,
With hands entwined, we forge ahead.
In every step, our bond so true,
On this path where hope is spread.

So let us dance through days unknown,
With courage fierce and spirits bright.
For in this journey, love has grown,
Echoes of joy, our guiding light.

Time's Gentle Touch

In quiet moments, time will speak,
The ticking clock, a tender friend.
With gentle hands, it molds the weak,
And guides us toward the journey's end.

Each fleeting hour, a precious gift,
In whispered secrets, stories flow.
Through every change, our hearts may lift,
Embracing all that we might know.

As seasons turn and years unfold,
We gather wisdom in our stride.
In memories rich and memories bold,
Time's gentle touch forever tied.

Through trials faced and joys we claim,
The moments shared, like threads of gold.
In every smile, in every name,
Time's gentle hand forever holds.

So let us cherish every beat,
For in this dance, our souls will find.
In time, the past and future meet,
A tapestry, both strong and kind.

The Ruins of Yesterday's Heart

In crumbling stone where dreams have gone,
Echoes linger of love once bright.
Through shadows cast by time's cruel dawn,
We search for remnants of the light.

Each cracked facade a tale retold,
Whispers of passion, now laid bare.
In ruins where the brave once strolled,
Ghosts of laughter fill the air.

Yet through the dust and faded hue,
A spark ignites in weary souls.
From ashes rise, a promise new,
In shattered hearts, the spirit rolls.

With every step on ancient ground,
We find the beauty in decay.
For even here, where loss is found,
Love's memory will never stray.

So let us build from what remains,
A world reborn from yesterday.
Amongst the ruins and the pains,
We'll find our strength, our own pathway.

Sunshine After the Storm

The clouds have drifted far away,
Golden rays begin to play.
Nature smiles with colors bright,
Restoring peace, embracing light.

Puddles glisten on the ground,
Whispers of joy in the sound.
Birds return, their songs sweet,
Life awakens, hearts will meet.

The trees stand tall, leaves anew,
Every drop, a fresh debut.
Tomorrow holds a brighter day,
Hope with each sunbeam on display.

Memories of the rain slowly fade,
In the warmth, our fears cascade.
Together we'll lift our eyes high,
Beneath the vast and open sky.

So let us dance in the golden hue,
Trusting in what we can renew.
For every storm has an end, you'll see,
Sunshine whispers, "Just be free."

The Cycle of Us

In spring we bloom, hearts in bloom,
Launch into love, dispel the gloom.
With laughter shared, hands entwined,
Two souls awakening, gently aligned.

Summer comes, warm and bright,
Long golden days, endless light.
Memories made beneath the stars,
Chasing dreams, erasing scars.

As autumn leaves begin to fall,
We gather round, hear the call.
Reflections shared in cozy nights,
Fueled by love's soft, warm lights.

Winter whispers, quiet and deep,
In its embrace, secrets we keep.
While frost sets in, our hearts ignite,
Together we brave the chill of night.

Through seasons' change, we stand as one,
Facing storms, basking in the sun.
In the cycle of us, love will thrive,
In each moment, we come alive.

Mending Through Time

Fragments scatter, lost in the past,
We gather pieces, finding at last.
With tender hands, we join each shard,
Creating a mosaic, healing each scar.

Through trials faced, we find our way,
In every heartbeat, a new sway.
Time stitches wounds with love untold,
Our stories woven, golden and bold.

In laughter and tears, we share our grace,
Each moment cherished, a warm embrace.
Together we build on memories fine,
In the art of mending through time.

With every dawn, we face the light,
Rebuilding dreams, taking flight.
Through every storm, shadows will fade,
And love's eternal bridge is made.

So fear not the cracks that we bear,
For in them lies the beauty we share.
Through time, we grow, together stronger,
In this tapestry, we last longer.

Rewoven Dreams

Threads of hope start to unwind,
In a fabric where dreams are entwined.
Each whisper of night holds a scheme,
As we gather fragments of every dream.

Stars above call out with grace,
Encouraging us to find our place.
With every stitch, our stories blend,
Mending the seams that never end.

Woven paths made by heart and hand,
Designs of love across this land.
In every color, our hopes alight,
A canvas bright against the night.

As we rework the threads we've spun,
The past embraced, the future begun.
Together we'll craft this tapestry wide,
In dreams rewoven, side by side.

So let the threads of fate entwine,
In every heartbeat, love will shine.
With courage steadfast, we'll weave anew,
In this dance of dreams, just me and you.

Rising from Ashes

In the silence, embers glow,
From the ruins, hope will grow.
Phoenix rises, wings spread wide,
From the darkness, dreams abide.

With each breath, a spark ignites,
Turning shadows into lights.
Amidst the scars, strength is found,
A testament, rising sound.

Through the struggle, hearts will soar,
A future blooms, evermore.
From the ashes, life will spring,
To the heavens, we will cling.

The past may haunt, yet we stand tall,
Embracing change, we heed the call.
Through the fire, we've been forged,
New beginnings, life enlarged.

In unity, let voices lift,
From despair, we find our gift.
Together strong, we face the dawn,
In the light, we're reborn.

The Heart's Refresh

Morning dew on petals bright,
Whispers soft in morning light.
With each beat, a gentle sigh,
Hearts awaken, time to fly.

Dreams once lost, now found anew,
Color embraces every hue.
With love's touch, the world transforms,
In the calm, the spirit warms.

Breath of spring in every sound,
Hope arises from the ground.
In this moment, we find peace,
With every heartache, a release.

Feel the rhythm, let it guide,
Open hearts, let love reside.
With each story shared among,
The heart's refresh, a vibrant song.

Together, we will journey far,
Chasing dreams, our guiding star.
In this dance of life, we see,
The heart's refresh, wild and free.

Notes from Yesterday

Faded pages, whispers soft,
Echoes linger, memories waft.
In the margins, truths unfold,
Tales of life, both brave and bold.

A word, a glance, a fleeting smile,
Moments captured, though for a while.
In the silence, stories breathe,
Building bridges, we believe.

The laughter shared, the tears we shed,
In every line, a life we've led.
Among the words, our spirits blend,
Yesterday's notes, a timeless friend.

As seasons change, so do the dreams,
Flowing gently, like moonbeams.
In the tapestry we weave,
Each thread carries what we believe.

Time may fade, yet love remains,
In the heart, no need for chains.
Notes from yesterday remind us still,
To cherish moments, to seek and feel.

A Serenade of Us

Under starlit skies so deep,
We find solace in the sweep.
A melody of heart and soul,
In harmony, we become whole.

With every note, love finds its way,
Creating magic, night or day.
In quiet whispers, feelings bloom,
Together, we light up the room.

Every glance, a symphony,
In this dance, we're wild and free.
With laughter, our spirits rise,
Chasing dreams beneath the skies.

Hands entwined, we face the night,
Guided by the soft moonlight.
With every heartbeat, our song unfolds,
A serenade of love it holds.

In this moment, let us be,
A timeless tune, you and me.
Together crafting love's sweet song,
In this serenade, we belong.

Threads of Connection

In a world of woven dreams,
Silent whispers pull the seams.
Every glance, a silent thread,
Binding hearts, where love is bred.

With each laugh, a stitch is sewn,
In warm embraces, we have grown.
Moments shared, they intertwine,
Creating paths, our souls align.

Through storms that come and go,
The strength of bonds continues to show.
In the fabric of our days,
Connection shines in countless ways.

The tapestry of lives we weave,
In shared hopes, we dare believe.
Across the miles, our hearts stay near,
In this dance, there's naught to fear.

Each thread tells a story true,
Of love and loss, of me and you.
In the art of life, we find our place,
Together woven, a warm embrace.

The Art of Together

Two souls painting skies of blue,
In every stroke, a bond so true.
Hand in hand, we face the day,
Together, we find our way.

With laughter bright and tears we share,
In every moment, love's the air.
In the quiet, in the loud,
Together we stand, strong and proud.

Through every joy and every trial,
Together we carry every mile.
In the canvas where dreams ignite,
We are bright stars against the night.

Each memory a brush, a hue,
Painting life with shades anew.
In the gallery of our embrace,
We capture time, we find our grace.

The art of together, bold and clear,
In every heartbeat, you are near.
In the masterpiece that we create,
Love is the brushstroke we cultivate.

Transitions in the Heart

Seasons change, like whispers soft,
In the heart, we drift aloft.
Through each dawn, new colors bloom,
Transitions weave through joy and gloom.

From spring's embrace to winter's chill,
The heart adapts, it learns its will.
In every heartbeat, we embrace,
The ebb and flow, this sacred space.

Moments shift like the rising tide,
In the journey, we learn to glide.
As autumn leaves begin to fall,
The heart finds strength within it all.

Each ending births a brand new start,
In the dance of life, we play our part.
Through every chapter, hand in hand,
We navigate this wondrous land.

Transitions paint the soul with grace,
In every change, we find our place.
With love as our compass, guiding true,
The heart remains steadfast, ever new.

A Heartbeat Reclaimed

In the silence, echoes restore,
A rhythm lost, now beats once more.
Through shadows deep, the light will beam,
A heartbeat wakes from a distant dream.

With every pulse, a tale is spun,
From broken paths, new journeys run.
In the stillness, courage blooms,
A heart reclaimed from fleeting glooms.

Through valleys low and mountains high,
We rise again, we touch the sky.
With every change, we find our way,
A heartbeat leads, come what may.

In moments raw, in feelings pure,
Love's gentle strength helps us endure.
Each breath we take, a promise made,
In every heartbeat, fears will fade.

A harmony in life unfolds,
In every beat, a story told.
From ashes, hope's bright flame will rise,
In a reclaimed heart, the spirit flies.

Dancing in the New Light

In the dawn's embrace we sway,
Floating on whispers ever bright,
Colors bloom with each soft ray,
Hearts entwined in pure delight.

Shadows fade as joy takes flight,
Every moment feels so right,
Footsteps harmonize tonight,
We are lost in the new light.

With the stars our guide above,
We explore the depths unknown,
Every twirl a dance of love,
In this space, we have grown.

The rhythm of our beating hearts,
Synchronizes under the moon,
In this dance, the magic starts,
Together, we make our tune.

As the music gently plays,
Through the night, we will abide,
In this sweet and tender gaze,
Forever, we shall not hide.

Love's Renaissance

In the garden where dreams grow,
Petals glisten with morning dew,
Seeds of hope begin to show,
Painting skies in shades of blue.

With each heartbeat, sparks ignite,
Old wounds mend, and spirits rise,
In the hush of tender night,
Rekindled by our love's sighs.

Whispers float upon the breeze,
Promises wrapped in velvet sound,
In this space, we're put at ease,
To each other, we are bound.

Every tear becomes a gem,
Shining bright through the endless pain,
Together, we rise again,
In love's dance, we'll never wane.

Hand in hand, we brave the storm,
With faith guiding every stride,
In our hearts, we feel the warm,
Light of love that won't divide.

The Return of Us

Time has woven its own tale,
Winding roads that led us far,
Yet our bond can never pale,
You're my compass, my North Star.

Through the trials, we held tight,
In the darkness, you were there,
With a fire burning bright,
Love's embrace beyond compare.

Now the world begins to fade,
As we step into the sun,
Each lost moment will cascade,
Into the joy we've just begun.

Every laugh and every tear,
Stacked like stones along our way,
Guiding paths that bring us near,
To the promise of today.

In each heartbeat, echoes stay,
Reminders of what's pure and true,
In the light, we'll laugh and play,
Together, forever, just us two.

Beyond the Horizon of Us

On the edge where skies collide,
And the sea greets the dawn's light,
In the silence, worlds abide,
Beyond horizons, pure delight.

Waves caress the sandy shore,
Carrying whispers from the past,
Every breeze opens a door,
To memories that hold us fast.

In the distance, dreams take flight,
Painting skies in hues of gold,
With each step, we claim our right,
To love in stories yet untold.

Crossing paths, we touch the stars,
With the universe as our guide,
Facing fears, no more scars,
In this love, we take our stride.

Together we'll chase the light,
Through every storm, we're not alone,
For within, our hearts unite,
Creating a world we call home.

Lifetimes Untangled

In shadows past, we roamed alone,
Among the whispers, seeds were sown.
Echoes meet where time stands still,
Our paths entwined by fate's own will.

Threads of laughter, pain, and grace,
In every life, we find our place.
Memories linger, soft and bright,
A tapestry born from shared light.

In myriad forms, love finds its way,
Through storms and sun, night and day.
We search the skies for signs anew,
In every heart, the past breaks through.

Together we weave, together we mend,
A journey endless, no start, no end.
Hands that once parted, now clasped tight,
In lifetimes untangled, we find our light.

With every heartbeat, echoes arise,
Reminders of what never dies.
In every lifetime, we learn to grow,
An eternal dance, in ebb and flow.

So let us sing, let voices soar,
For love transcends, forevermore.
In the fabric of time, may we reside,
With lifetimes untangled, side by side.

The Dance of Reconnection

In twilight's glow, we meet again,
Old friends in echoes, never plain.
With every step, our hearts align,
In the dance of life, a sacred sign.

Time has spun its gentle thread,
In silence spoken, words unsaid.
With eyes that shine like stars above,
We twirl and sway, a tale of love.

Together we breathe, a rhythmic beat,
In the soft embrace where souls do meet.
Our laughter floats like petals in air,
In this dance, we shed our care.

Through twists and turns, we've grown so bright,
In shadows cast, we find the light.
The past may linger, but here we stand,
In the dance of reconnection, hand in hand.

With every falter, we rise anew,
A circle formed by me and you.
On this sacred floor, we shall remain,
In the dance of life, joy and pain.

So let us twirl, let spirits fly,
In rhythms known, beneath the sky.
Together we'll weave a story true,
In the dance of reconnection, just we two.

A Love Illuminated

In the quiet dusk, your eyes ignite,
A spark of warmth, a soothing light.
Through whispered dreams in starlit skies,
A world transformed when love replies.

Each moment shared, a treasure found,
In laughter's echo, love is crowned.
With gentle touch, the heart will sway,
In this embrace, we'll find our way.

Through turbulent seas and calm so grand,
Together we walk, hand in hand.
In depths of night, our souls take flight,
A love illuminated, bold and bright.

With every dawn, new colors bloom,
In your embrace, the shadows loom.
A canvas painted with hues of glee,
In love's warm grasp, we are set free.

So let us shine, two stars aligned,
In this universe, forever entwined.
In moments fleeting, our breath is shared,
A love illuminated, a heart laid bare.

Reviving the Flame

In the quiet night, embers glow,
Flickering softly, whispers slow.
Through winds of change, we felt the chill,
Yet in our hearts, the spark was still.

With gentle words, we fan the fire,
Rekindling dreams and deep desire.
In shadows past, love softly fades,
Yet here we stand, unafraid.

Through trials faced and lessons learned,
In every twist, our passion burned.
Like phoenix rising, we will reclaim,
The warmth alive, reviving the flame.

Let's gather close, with hands held tight,
As moonlight bathes the endless night.
In tender moments, we find our way,
With love as guide, we'll never sway.

So here's to us, a bond renewed,
Through all the storms, through all we've viewed.
In hearts united, we'll stand the test,
Reviving the flame, eternally blessed.

Heartbeats Under the Same Sky

Under the veil of the night,
Our hearts dance in soft light.
Whispers carried by the breeze,
Binding souls in quiet ease.

Stars shimmer like distant dreams,
In the silence, hope redeems.
Every heartbeat hums a tune,
Beneath the watchful moon.

In this moment, time stands still,
Magic flows with every thrill.
Holding hands, we face the dark,
Together igniting a spark.

As the dawn begins to break,
Promises we softly make.
In the glow of morning's rise,
We remain, love never lies.

Together, under this expanse,
Life turns into a chance.
Forever beats a loving heart,
In this world, never apart.

Evenings of Anew

The sun dips low, painting skies,
In hues that catch the wary eyes.
Each evening whispers tales of old,
New stories waiting to unfold.

Shadows stretch across the ground,
In silence, peace is softly found.
Crickets sing a lullaby,
As gentle breezes pass us by.

Hand in hand, we seek the light,
Filling hearts with pure delight.
Every evening brings a chance,
To rediscover love's romance.

With every star, wishes bloom,
Chasing away the lingering gloom.
In the twilight, dreams take flight,
Guided by the moon's soft light.

Together we stand, unbroken,
In our hearts, words left unspoken.
Evenings blend into forever,
In this journey, we are tethered.

The Chorus of Together Again

Voices rise in harmony,
A chorus sings in jubilee.
Each note strummed is a tale,
Tales of love that shall not pale.

In unison, we find our way,
United in the light of day.
Together, we face the storm,
In your arms, I am reborn.

The melody wraps us tight,
Guiding us through darkest night.
Every heartbeat, every sound,
In this rhythm, hope is found.

As the echoes softly swell,
Our stories weave a magic spell.
Together, we dance once more,
On this journey, love will soar.

In the chorus, we belong,
With every moment, we are strong.
Together again, hand in hand,
In this song, we make our stand.

Fragments of Us: The Restoration

In pieces, we were scattered wide,
Yet love held through every tide.
With gentle hands, we start to mend,
Restoring what we once did send.

Every fragment tells a story,
Of joy, of pain, and quiet glory.
In the cracks, beauty will rise,
Through the tears, we find our ties.

Rebuilding dreams, one by one,
In the darkness, we find the sun.
Together, we stitch the seams,
Daring to live out our dreams.

In this garden, hearts take root,
From the struggle, blooms the fruit.
With every step, we learn to thrive,
In fragments, we find our drive.

Through shattered paths, we walk anew,
In each other, we see the view.
Restoration of our core,
In love's embrace, we will soar.

Tides of Togetherness

In the dawn, we rise anew,
With hearts entwined, a vibrant hue.
Through storms we sail, not alone,
Together strong, a love we've grown.

Moments shared, like waves they crash,
In laughter's echo, memories flash.
With every tide, we find our way,
In unity, we choose to stay.

Hand in hand, we face the sun,
With every battle, we have won.
Infinite skies, our dreams take flight,
In every dusk, we find our light.

As seasons shift, so do we learn,
In every corner, love's deep burn.
With open hearts, we face the night,
Together always, our shared light.

In the ebb, in the flow, we trust,
In every whisper, it's love or bust.
Through life's vast ocean, we will roam,
In tides of togetherness, we find home.

Holding the Light

In shadows deep, we search for grace,
A flicker shines in a daunting space.
With tender hands, we hold it tight,
Guiding our way through darkest night.

Each step we take, a chance we find,
With hope's bright glow, our hearts aligned.
Through trials fierce, our spirits soar,
In unity, we're so much more.

A bond unbroken, like stars above,
Illuminates the path of love.
With every heartbeat, we ignite,
A burning flame, our shared delight.

Embracing change, we rise and fall,
In kindness wrapped, we heed the call.
Together, dear, we'll face the fight,
In every shadow, we hold the light.

As daylight fades, new dreams awake,
In gentle whispers, love won't break.
Together shining, bold and bright,
In all we do, we hold the light.

In the Arms of Change

When leaves turn gold and skies grow dim,
In change, we find what's true within.
A dance of time, a gentle sway,
In the arms of change, we learn to play.

With every season, lessons learned,
In quiet moments, passion burned.
We wrap ourselves in soft embrace,
Finding strength in every space.

Tides may shift, and paths may bend,
Yet through it all, we learn to mend.
In uncertainty, our hearts engage,
Forever safe in the arms of change.

As dawn unveils a brand new day,
We step with grace, come what may.
In every ending, a chance to start,
In the warmth of change, we find our heart.

Through trials faced, we rise and flow,
In every heartbeat, love will grow.
Together strong, we take the stage,
In the beauty found in the arms of change.

Sketches of Affection

With every stroke, the canvas speaks,
In vibrant hues, our passion peaks.
Soft whispers dance in colors bright,
In sketches drawn, we find our light.

A gentle touch, a loving glance,
In simple gestures, our hearts prance.
The art of love, it's rich and rare,
In every frame, a memory shared.

Lines interwoven, stories told,
In every detail, a love bold.
With every sketch, we capture time,
In affection's frame, our hearts climb.

Through shades of joy and hues of pain,
In every portrait, love remains.
With colors blending, we define,
In sketches of affection, you're mine.

As seasons shift, we still create,
In every moment, love's our fate.
Together crafting, hand in hand,
In life's grand gallery, we shall stand.

Rekindled Promises

In shadows deep, we find the light,
Whispers soft in the still of night.
With every tear, a dream reborn,
Together now, we'll brave the storm.

Promises made beneath the stars,
Every heartbeat, healing scars.
Hand in hand, our fears set free,
In your eyes, I find my peace.

Time has passed, but love endures,
Through fragile hearts, the glow ensures.
With every dawn, a chance to grow,
In rekindled vows, our passion flows.

Through winding paths and twisted fates,
We navigate those heavy gates.
In laughter shared, in moments true,
A world reborn, just me and you.

So take my hand, let's write our tale,
Against the winds, we will not fail.
With every promise, strong and bright,
We'll build our dreams in morning light.

Dreams Intertwined

In twilight hush, our visions blend,
A tapestry that never ends.
In whispered dreams, we dance as one,
Chasing shadows 'til the sun.

Through starlit skies, our wishes call,
In soft embrace, we rise and fall.
Each heartbeat syncs with fate's design,
In every glance, our souls align.

With every step, our paths unite,
Bound by love, we sparkle bright.
In fields of gold, we roam anew,
Crafting life from shades of blue.

Silent prayers on whispered winds,
In every journey, joy begins.
With open hearts, we seek the signs,
In dreams we share, our spirits shine.

So let us wander, hand in hand,
In this vast and wondrous land.
Together strong, we'll face the night,
In dreams entwined, our hearts take flight.

Echoing Footsteps

In quiet halls where memories thrive,
Echoing footsteps bring the past alive.
Whispers linger in the air,
Stories shared, hearts laid bare.

With every step on polished floor,
We recall the laughter, the love we wore.
Through open doors, we see the light,
Guiding us through the fall of night.

In every corner, a piece remains,
Of fleeting joys and hidden pains.
But in the echoes, hope is found,
A symphony of love profound.

Beneath the weight of the years gone by,
We chart our course through a troubled sky.
In the rhythm of hearts, we'll carry forth,
With echoing footsteps, we'll find our worth.

So as we walk these paths so dear,
Together, love will conquer fear.
In every echo, a promise true,
With footsteps united, just me and you.

A Revival of Affection

In soft glows of a dying sun,
We find the warmth where love begun.
In gentle smiles and tender sighs,
Awakening the heart's replies.

Time stood still when you held me close,
A moment frozen, the sweetest dose.
In every laugh, in every tear,
A revival of affection draws near.

Through winding roads of joy and strife,
We gather strength, reignite our life.
Unfurl the dreams we once let fade,
In moments shared, the memories wade.

With every touch, the flame ignites,
In long-lost nights and starry flights.
Through echoes of our past we tread,
In whispered hopes, new dreams are bred.

So take my heart and hold it tight,
Through every shadow, we'll find the light.
In this revival, forever true,
In love's embrace, it's me and you.

Reflections in the Waters of Time

In quiet streams the echoes flow,
Whispers of dreams we used to know.
Moments captured, lost in hue,
Ripples dance to memories true.

Beneath the surface, shadows play,
Mirrored thoughts of yesterday.
In each reflection, tales unfold,
Stories of the brave and bold.

Time's gentle touch, a tender art,
We weave our past within our heart.
Like falling leaves in autumn's grace,
Each memory finds its rightful place.

The river winds, a path of fate,
Between the stones, we navigate.
Each twist and turn reveals a sign,
Connecting threads through waters fine.

So pause a while, and watch the flow,
In stillness, learn what time can show.
Embrace the echoes, hold them dear,
In every ripple, love appears.

A Fusion of Old and New

In bustling streets where cultures blend,
Old stories meet the new trend.
From ancient paths to modern ways,
We find our light in brighter days.

The clink of glass, the scent of spice,
Traditions rich adorn our slice.
Through every laugh, a song we hear,
A tapestry of hope and cheer.

Wisdom flows from those before,
Guiding us to open doors.
In every heart, a burning flame,
The past and future, never the same.

Hand in hand, we build and grow,
With each small step, we pave our glow.
The canvas broadens, colors bright,
In perfect harmony, day and night.

So raise a toast to all we share,
To dreams and visions found in prayer.
For in this dance of old and new,
We shape a world, forever true.

Shores of Hope Revisited

Upon the sand, we write our dreams,
Each wave a whisper, each tide a theme.
Footprints fade, but hope remains,
In these shores, joy over pains.

The horizon beckons, bright and clear,
With every sunrise, we conquer fear.
The gulls in flight, a freedom song,
In unity, we all belong.

Seashells gather stories untold,
Each polished reminder of dreams bold.
With every tide, we find our ground,
In the rhythm of waves, love is found.

As dusk settles, colors entwine,
A canvas painted, pure divine.
Each star above, a guiding light,
A promise kept through darkest night.

So walk these shores, hand in hand,
With hearts attuned to life's grand plan.
In every grain, the hopes we weave,
In the sands of time, we shall believe.

A Compass to Each Other's Hearts

In whispered winds, a calling clear,
A compass guides us near and dear.
Through storms and calm, we find our way,
In every dawn, love leads the day.

With every heartbeat, trust we mold,
In laughter shared, our stories told.
Across each distance, bonds we tie,
With open hearts, we learn to fly.

Through valleys low and mountains high,
Together we soar, together we try.
With every sunset, dreams ignite,
In shared ambitions, our spirits light.

The map we chart, a journey vast,
In every moment, shadows cast.
In the compass rose of our embrace,
We find our truth, our gentle space.

So take my hand, let's navigate,
With hearts aligned, we'll chart our fate.
In love's direction, we'll forever steer,
A compass guiding, always near.

Reigniting the Spark

In shadows deep, where dreams reside,
A flicker glows, the flame inside.
With gentle hands, we fan the fire,
Awakening hearts, igniting desire.

Memories dance like stars above,
Each laugh a note, a song of love.
We breathe new life, our spirits soar,
In every glance, we seek for more.

Through whispered words, we find our way,
In twilight's hue, we choose to stay.
With every heartbeat, passion's song,
Together, where we both belong.

The moments shared, like threads, entwine,
A tapestry of joy, divine.
In every touch, a spark ignites,
In this embrace, our souls unite.

So here we stand, hand in hand,
With courage strong, we make our stand.
Reigniting flames that gently glow,
In love's great dance, we'll ever grow.

Moments Reimagined

In quiet corners, time unfolds,
A story rich, like dreams retold.
Each moment cherished, vivid, bright,
We paint our past in colors light.

Through laughter shared and tears that flow,
In every second, love will grow.
We turn the page, a fresh new start,
Reimagining what's in our heart.

With open arms, we greet the dawn,
New paths await, the past is gone.
In every breath, we find our cheer,
Moments reimagined, precious, clear.

We dance to rhythms only we know,
And in our hearts, the laughter will flow.
With courage found in each embrace,
A journey set, our sacred space.

So let us weave our dreams anew,
In every moment, me and you.
With love as our guiding light,
Moments reimagined, pure delight.

Whispers of the Heart

In the stillness, soft winds sigh,
Whispers of love that never die.
Each secret shared, a fragile thread,
Connecting souls, where fears are shed.

The heart's soft song, a gentle call,
Through shadows deep, we rise and fall.
In every glance, a story spun,
Two souls entwined, forever one.

With tender words that brush the night,
We weave our dreams with purest light.
In quiet moments, we understand,
The whispers guide, a steady hand.

In the chaos, peace we find,
A dance of souls, our hearts aligned.
With every heartbeat, faith renewed,
Whispers of hope, our love pursued.

So let us listen to the sound,
Of whispers soft, where love is found.
In every silence, truth imparts,
The timeless echoes of our hearts.

The Bridge We Build

Across the river, wide and deep,
A bridge we build, our promises keep.
With dreams as strong as iron steel,
Together, we create, we feel.

Each stone we lay, a memory made,
With laughter shared, foundations laid.
Through trials faced, our spirits shine,
In unity, our hearts entwine.

With open arms, we greet the day,
On this bridge of love, we find our way.
Hand in hand, we cross with grace,
In every step, our sacred space.

Through storms that rage and skies that clear,
This bridge will hold, we'll persevere.
With every heartbeat, every sigh,
Together, we will learn to fly.

So let us walk this path we choose,
On the bridge we build, we cannot lose.
With love as our guide, we'll always find,
The strength to stand, our hearts aligned.

Whispers of Reconnection

Lost in the silence, we find our way,
Soft echoes of laughter, where shadows play.
A gentle reminder that love still thrives,
The heart's quiet whispers, where hope survives.

Through winding paths, we stroll once more,
Opening doors to what we adore.
With every heartbeat, a story unfolds,
In the realm of the brave, our truth is told.

Moments forgotten, yet not misplaced,
In the tapestry woven, we'll find our grace.
Each thread a memory, entwined so fine,
A dance of connections, forever divine.

With open arms, we embrace the past,
In the warmth of reunion, our hearts hold fast.
An unbroken bond that time can't sever,
In whispers of love, we linger forever.

The Flame Rekindles

In the darkness, a spark remains,
Flickering softly, as love reclaims.
From ashes of silence, hope starts to grow,
A radiant warmth, an ember's glow.

With every glance, the flame builds high,
Illuminating dreams, as shadows fly.
A dance of desire ignites the night,
Together we soar, with hearts alight.

Words left unspoken now find their voice,
Through fire and passion, we make our choice.
Casting aside what held us apart,
With courage and love, we rekindle our heart.

Through trials faced, our spirits unite,
Two souls intertwined, in love's pure light.
A journey reborn, through laughter and tears,
In the warmth of the flame, we conquer our fears.

Tender Threads of Time

In moments of stillness, we weave our fate,
With tender threads, we patiently wait.
Each stitch a promise, each knot a vow,
In the fabric of life, we cherish the now.

Time is a river, flowing so slow,
Carving our paths where memories grow.
We gather our stories, reflect on the years,
In every heartbeat, a tapestry of tears.

Through sunlit days and shadowed nights,
We hold onto love, in our precious sights.
A gentle reminder, in laughter's embrace,
The beauty of time, we lovingly trace.

With every sunrise, new threads intertwine,
In the garden of life, our blossoms align.
Nurtured with care, our spirits will climb,
In the cradle of moments, we dance through time.

Serendipity's Dance

In a chance encounter, worlds shift and sway,
Two hearts collide, in an unexpected play.
With every stumble, a new tale unfolds,
In serendipity's grip, our fate it holds.

A smile exchanged, a look in the eyes,
Fate's gentle whisper as the moment flies.
With laughter and joy, we twirl through the night,
In the rhythm of fate, our spirits take flight.

Underneath the stars, we find our way,
Guided by wishes that won't fade away.
Each twist of the dance, a spark of delight,
In serendipity's arms, everything feels right.

With every chance meeting, new journeys start,
Creating connections that warm the heart.
In this wondrous dance, we lose and we find,
In serendipity's weave, our souls are entwined.

A Hearth Rekindled

In the twilight glow of evening,
Flickers of warmth reappear.
Memories dance in the shadows,
Whispers of love draw near.

Logs crackle as stories unfold,
Echoes of laughter fill the air.
With each flame, a tale retold,
Hearts entwined, a bond so rare.

The scent of pine, a soft embrace,
Bringing solace as night descends.
Time slows down in this sacred space,
Where the heartache softly mends.

Gathered here, we find our home,
In the warmth that light ignites.
No longer do we face the chrome,
For together, we reach new heights.

A hearth rekindled, flames that glow,
Igniting dreams we thought had ceased.
In this sanctuary, love will grow,
A promise kept, our souls released.

Under the Moonlit Promise

Beneath the stars, our hearts ignite,
Under the moon, a tender trance.
Whispers weave through the silent night,
As shadows stretch in a secret dance.

The silver beams caress your face,
Lighting up dreams we dare to share.
In this world, we find our place,
A moment lost, beyond compare.

Gentle breezes softly sway,
Rustling leaves in a sweet embrace.
Here, time stands still, a starlit play,
Two souls intertwined in space.

With every sigh, the night unfolds,
Our laughter ringing through the air.
In this promise, our love beholds,
The magic found, beyond despair.

Together, we chase the dawn anew,
With every step, the shadows fade.
In this dance, my heart is true,
Under the moon, our dreams are made.

Shadows Cast by Our Laughter

In the twilight, shadows grow long,
Echoes of laughter fill the night.
With whispers sweet, we sing our song,
Creating joy, a radiant light.

Each chuckle dances in the air,
Making memories, we hold so dear.
In the night, our spirits bare,
Finding solace, free from fear.

Playful jests weave through the crowd,
As hearts unite beneath the stars.
No worries here can feel too loud,
In this moment, we heal our scars.

Together we stand, hand in hand,
Casting shadows that fade away.
In laughter's embrace, we find our land,
A cherished space where love will stay.

With every giggle, we break the night,
Binding the gaps with threads of cheer.
In laughter's warmth, our hearts take flight,
Creating bonds that last all year.

Alighting on Familiar Shores

Upon the tide, we start to roam,
Finding peace where waves do crash.
Each step we take, it feels like home,
On golden sands, the hours flash.

Footprints trace where we have been,
In laughter lost to ocean's hum.
Memories dance, like waves we swim,
To the beat of hearts where rhythms come.

Gulls cry out in a playful way,
As we weave dreams in the salty air.
In this moment, we choose to stay,
Finding solace, beyond compare.

The horizon holds our whispered dreams,
In every splash, we hear love's song.
Together we build, or so it seems,
A life where we both belong.

As sunset paints the sky aglow,
We savor sunsets, hand in hand.
Alighting here on familiar shores,
With every heartbeat, we understand.

A Garden in the Making

Seeds are sown with care and love,
Beneath the sky so bright above.
They whisper dreams of blooms to be,
In colors bold, wild, and free.

Sunlight dances on the ground,
While gentle breezes swirl around.
Each petal bears a tale to tell,
Of growth, of joy, of living well.

Water trickles, quenching thirst,
Nurturing life, a joyous burst.
In every leaf, a story grows,
Of trials faced and hope that glows.

As time unfolds, the garden thrives,
In harmony, where beauty drives.
A canvas painted by the hand,
Of nature's grace in fertile land.

With patient heart, we tend with care,
A sacred space, a love to share.
In this garden, dreams take flight,
Reflecting all that's pure and right.

From Ashes, We Bloom

From ashes deep, we rise anew,
With strength forged from the trials we rue.
Like phoenix wings in vibrant flight,
We find our way from darkest night.

Each scar a mark of battles won,
Each tear a glimpse of rising sun.
In every shadow, there shines a spark,
A flicker of hope igniting the dark.

The roots run deep, through pain and strife,
In woven threads, we find our life.
Determined hearts embrace the wind,
For from the loss, new dreams begin.

We bloom with colors bold and bright,
Reclaiming joy, embracing light.
With every petal, we breathe in grace,
Transforming scars into embrace.

Though paths be rough, and storms may come,
We stand as one, the beating drum.
From ashes warm, we rise, we soar,
In unity, forevermore.

Starlit Paths to Reconnection

Beneath the stars, we walk as one,
In whispers soft, our hearts are spun.
The night unveils a sacred dance,
In dreams awakened, lost in chance.

With every step, the shadows fade,
As memories rise from the cascade.
We share our stories, tales of old,
In starlit paths, our souls unfold.

The universe sings in gentle ways,
Guiding us through life's maze.
With laughter shared and hopes reborn,
In twilight's glow, new paths adorn.

Hand in hand, through uncharted skies,
We forge anew, where love never dies.
In every heartbeat, the echo calls,
Of reconnection that never falls.

In starlit nights, we find our way,
Through every word and soft ballet.
We are the stars, forever bright,
Guiding each other toward the light.

Echoes of Laughter and Light

In playful echoes, laughter rings,
A melody of joy that sings.
With every smile that brightly gleams,
We weave together cherished dreams.

The sunlight dances on our cheeks,
As stories shared fill quiet peaks.
In gentle hugs and whispered grace,
We build a warm, familiar space.

Moments captured, forever dear,
Each note of laughter, crystal clear.
Through ups and downs, we stand as one,
In life's theater, our hearts outrun.

In every tear, a glimmer shines,
Of love that flows and intertwines.
With open hearts, we greet the day,
In echoes sweet, our troubles sway.

Through stormy nights and sunny skies,
We find our strength, our spirits rise.
In laughter's arms, we find delight,
As echoes linger, pure and bright.

Echoes of Our Togetherness

In the quiet of the night,
Whispers dance like firelight.
Memories wane, yet remain,
Binding us with gentle chains.

Laughter rings through the halls,
Echoes of our earnest calls.
Moments lost in time's embrace,
Yet in heart, they find their place.

Seasons change and time will flow,
Yet the bond we hold will grow.
Through the storms and sunny days,
Together, we'll find our ways.

In every shadow, in each sun,
Our journey weaves, two become one.
Hand in hand through thick and thin,
In this life, our hearts begin.

Forever etched, our story's art,
Two souls beat, no need to part.
Together through all life's test,
In each echo, we are blessed.

A Love Reawakened

In the stillness of the dawn,
Old memories start to yawn.
Whispers float on morning air,
A spark ignites, so rich, so rare.

Eyes that meet across the room,
Flickers spark, dispelling gloom.
Words once lost find voice again,
In this dance, our hearts begin.

Moments shared over time's flow,
The seeds of love begin to grow.
In the laughter, in the sigh,
A love reawakened will not die.

With every heartbeat, feelings swell,
In your arms, I find my bell.
Harmony in every glance,
In your presence, I find my chance.

Together we build our dream,
Life flows like a gentle stream.
In every second, love's embrace,
A reawakened, timeless space.

Pathways in Bloom

Beneath the sky so vast and blue,
Trail of colors comes into view.
Petals dance in the soft spring breeze,
Nature's song puts the heart at ease.

Each pathway lined with fragrant rose,
Unfolding tales that everyone knows.
A journey where laughter fills the air,
With every step, we feel the care.

Life, like gardens, blooms and fades,
Through the sun and soft cascades.
In each bloom, a story unfolds,
In nature's hands, warmth it holds.

Hands entwined, we walk this road,
Finding joy in our shared load.
Each petal whispers sweet delight,
Together we will chase the light.

Pathways in bloom, a vibrant scene,
In the beauty, we've always been.
With every breath, our spirits rise,
In this garden, love never dies.

Embracing Change

Seasons shift, the world will turn,
With every loss, there's more to learn.
Leaves will fall, yet roots remain,
In this cycle, there's no pain.

The river flows, it twists and bends,
Change is where our spirit mends.
From shadows deep to brightened skies,
In every ending, a new sunrise.

Paths may wind through thick and thin,
Each shift invites a fresh begin.
Embracing lessons, strong and wise,
Rising up to claim the prize.

In letting go, we find our grace,
Transforming hearts in every space.
With courage fierce, we take our stand,
Together, we can face what's planned.

Embracing change is not a fear,
It's the dawn that draws us near.
Through every twist, we'll find the way,
In this dance, we'll always stay.

Threads of Tomorrow

In the loom of dawn we weave,
Dreams that the heart can believe.
Colors bright, tales untold,
Future's fabric starts to unfold.

With every stitch, hope threads tight,
Guiding us through day and night.
Woven paths and tangled seams,
Hold the promise of our dreams.

Through the storms and sunlit skies,
Each thread carries whispered cries.
In vibrant hues, we find our way,
Threads of tomorrow shape today.

Together we spin, together we bind,
A tapestry rich, uniquely designed.
With love's embrace, we create our fate,
Threads of tomorrow, a bond innate.

So let the needle pierce the fabric,
Charting journeys, some exotic.
For in this craft, we find our worth,
Threads of tomorrow, heralds of earth.

The Canvas of Togetherness

In soft hues of laughter and light,
We paint our dreams, bold and bright.
Every stroke tells a story anew,
The canvas sings of me and you.

With colors mixed, our hearts unite,
In the glow of the shared delight.
Blending shades, our spirits twine,
Creating art, uniquely divine.

Brush and palette, hand in hand,
We journey forth in this sacred land.
Through highs and lows, we find our way,
On this canvas, night and day.

Each splash of paint, a memory's mark,
In vibrant whispers, we leave our spark.
Together we stand, forever entwined,
In the canvas of togetherness, love defined.

As seasons change and time does flow,
Our masterpiece continues to grow.
In every corner, a tale unfolds,
The canvas of togetherness, a treasure of gold.

Starlit Memories

Under the vast and shimmering sky,
We capture moments that never die.
Memories twinkle, like stars aligned,
In the night's embrace, our hearts combined.

Whispers of laughter, echoes of pain,
In the starlit dance, we rise again.
Every gleam holds the stories we wrote,
A constellation of dreams we tote.

Through twilight's glow and morning's embrace,
Starlit memories, time cannot erase.
In the gentle silence, we reminisce,
Finding comfort in every bliss.

With each flicker, a wish takes flight,
Guided by love, our guiding light.
Together we'll walk on paths of dreams,
In starlit memories, life, it seems.

So let us gather the stars so bright,
And weave them in our hearts tonight.
For in every shimmer, our essence stays,
In starlit memories, forever ablaze.

Unfolding the Past

In pages worn and whispers low,
The tales of yesteryears softly glow.
Each memory a thread in the weave,
Unfolding the past, we dare to believe.

With gentle hands, we turn each leaf,
Finding solace in stories of grief.
A tapestry rich with laughter and tears,
Unfolding the past, honoring our fears.

In the ink of time, our truths emerge,
Navigating paths where feelings surge.
Lessons learned in shadows cast,
In the journey of life, we hold our past.

From every trial, a strength is born,
In the dawn of wisdom, we rise each morn.
With open hearts, we stand steadfast,
Embracing the journey, unfolding the past.

So let us cherish the scars that remain,
For in their presence, we find our gain.
In the echoes of time, we find our part,
Unfolding the past, a work of art.

Beyond the Shadows of Yesterday

In whispers soft, the past awakes,
Memories linger, like water's breaks.
A dawn that shines on weary eyes,
Hope unfurls as darkness flies.

Footsteps echo on the ground,
In silence lost, new strength is found.
Each breath brings a chance to mend,
The scars of time we start to mend.

Through valleys deep, emotions flow,
With every heartbeat, seeds we sow.
The strength of now, a beacon bright,
Guides us gently into light.

Beyond the veil, a future gleams,
Where yesterday's haze dissolves in dreams.
A path awaits with open arms,
Embracing change with all its charms.

Let shadows fade and spirits rise,
In unity, we claim the skies.
With courage found in every song,
We write our tale, where we belong.

Blooming in Harmony

In gardens where the sunbeams play,
Petals dance in bright array.
Colors blend, a joyous sight,
Nature sings in pure delight.

Each blossom tells a story true,
Of whispered dreams and morning dew.
Together we create a song,
In harmony, where we belong.

The fragrant breeze, a gentle guide,
Through fields of hope, we walk side by side.
In every hue, a love declared,
In unity, our hearts are bared.

As seasons change, we hold on tight,
Embracing life's unfolding light.
Each moment shared, a sweet refrain,
Together in joys and pains.

Blooming forth in vibrant grace,
We find our place in nature's embrace.
In every petal, love we weave,
In harmony, we learn to believe.

The Palette of Us

In strokes of color, life unfolds,
A canvas rich, our story told.
With every hue, emotions blend,
In shades of love, we transcend.

A splash of joy, a hint of pain,
Together we compose the rain.
With midnight blue and sunlit gold,
In every brush, our hearts are bold.

From quiet pastels to vibrant tones,
We cherish whispers, soft and alone.
In laughter bright, in tears that flow,
The palette of us begins to grow.

With every layer, depth we find,
A masterpiece of heart and mind.
Through storms and calm, we paint the sky,
In colors true, we learn to fly.

So let's embrace this art we share,
A tapestry of love and care.
With every stroke, we'll build anew,
The palette of us, me and you.

A Symphony Replayed

In echoes soft, the music swells,
A symphony of whispered spells.
With every note, our hearts align,
In harmony, our spirits shine.

The rhythm flows like gentle streams,
In every chord, a world of dreams.
Together we compose the dance,
Entranced by fate, we take our chance.

Through crescendos, our voices rise,
In melodies, we find the skies.
With every beat, we weave a tune,
An endless song beneath the moon.

In softer tones, the heart does speak,
A symphony of love unique.
With every pause, a breath we share,
In silence found, we show we care.

So let the music play once more,
In every note, our spirits soar.
A symphony that will not fade,
In love's embrace, our song is made.

The Alchemy of Us

In the silence, we found our gold,
Each whispered secret, a story told.
Two hearts merging, a sacred trust,
In the fires of passion, we turn to dust.

As stardust mingles, we become whole,
Transforming shadows, igniting the soul.
You are the flame, and I am the spark,
Together igniting love's sweet arc.

Through trials we bend, never we break,
In this alchemy, a bond we make.
With every heartbeat, with every sigh,
We weave our dreams across the sky.

We dance through time, in laughter we spin,
A timeless embrace where love can begin.
Each tender glance, a potion pure,
In the alchemy of us, we endure.

So let us craft our magic bright,
In the night's embrace, our hearts take flight.
With you, my love, forever I'll be,
In this alchemy, just you and me.

Petals of Promise

In gardens where dreams softly sway,
Each petal whispers what words can't say.
Beneath the light of the crescent moon,
Hope unfurls in a fragrant tune.

With every bloom, a promise made,
In vibrant hues that never fade.
Together we nurture, together we grow,
Through stormy days and the sun's warm glow.

The fragrance of love, so sweet and pure,
In each gentle moment, our hearts endure.
As we gather moments, fragile and bright,
In the garden of us, a beautiful sight.

With hands intertwined, we plant our dreams,
In the fertile soil, nothing is as it seems.
A tapestry woven with colors that last,
In the petals of promise, our shadows are cast.

So let the winds carry our laughter far,
In the blossoms of love, our guiding star.
With each dawn, a renewal we see,
In this garden of hope, just you and me.

A Journey Back to Us

Winding paths through the trees so tall,
Echoes of laughter, a distant call.
In the rustling leaves, we find our way,
A journey back to love's bright day.

Through valleys deep and mountains high,
Together we wander, just you and I.
Every step taken, hand in hand,
In this sacred journey, we understand.

The stories we carry, the dreams we hold,
In the tapestry of time, our hearts unfold.
With every sunset, a chance to renew,
This journey back leads me to you.

Beneath the stars, we share our dreams,
In the twilight glow, your laughter beams.
Through the whispers of night, I feel your touch,
In this journey back, I cherish so much.

Though the road may twist and the skies may gray,
In the warmth of your gaze, I long to stay.
As we travel on, may our love thrive,
In this journey back, together we strive.

The Reawakening of Longing

From distant shores, a memory stirs,
A whispering breeze, the heart concurs.
In the quiet corners, shadows bloom,
The reawakening dispels the gloom.

With every heartbeat, desire ignites,
In the stillness of night, love takes flight.
Echoes of passion, a lingering sign,
In the depths of longing, your heart is mine.

The dance of the fire, the flicker of light,
In this reawakening, everything's right.
We chase the moments that time forgot,
In hidden places, our love is sought.

Through the tapestry woven by hands of fate,
We embrace the feelings that never abate.
With the fervor of dawn, our spirits bloom,
In the reawakening, love finds room.

So come, my dear, let's savor the night,
With each whispered word, let our souls unite.
In this sweet reverie, let longing play,
In the reawakening, we'll always stay.

Whispers of the Heart's Revival

In shadows soft, the whispers call,
A gentle breeze, we rise and fall.
With every breath, new hope ignites,
Reviving dreams in starry nights.

As petals dance on morning's light,
We find our way, hearts taking flight.
The rhythm of love, a sweet refrain,
In every joy, there's room for pain.

Through tangled paths, our spirits weave,
In silent vows, we both believe.
Each glance we share, a sacred thread,
A tapestry from words unsaid.

Like rivers merge and oceans meet,
Your heartbeat's pulse, my soul's retreat.
Together, strong, we'll face the tide,
In whispers soft, our love won't hide.

With every dawn, a chance renewed,
In love's embrace, we are imbued.
The heart revives in sacred trust,
In whispers soft, we rise from dust.

Echoes of Our Embrace

Beneath the moon, our laughter flows,
In twilight's grasp, our love still grows.
With every sigh, a promise sweet,
In echoes soft, our hearts will meet.

The night unfolds, a canvas vast,
With memories built to ever last.
In each embrace, we find our grace,
Returning home, to love's warm place.

Through every storm, we stand as one,
Two souls entwined, not coming undone.
Your gentle touch, a soothing balm,
In chaos loud, you're always calm.

In whispered words, we seal our fate,
With every heartbeat, we elevate.
Together we rise, in dreams we chase,
In every breath, an endless space.

So let us dance beneath the stars,
In echoes soft, our love is ours.
With every step, your hand in mine,
In endless night, our hearts align.

A Dance of Second Chances

Amidst the ruins, hope lies bare,
In shattered dreams, we find our dare.
Together we weave, a chance reborn,
In every dusk, a brighter morn.

Step lightly now, the rhythm sways,
Through darkness fades, our light conveys.
With open hearts, we take the floor,
In perfect time, we crave for more.

Each stumble leads to grace anew,
In every fall, there's strength in two.
With every twirl, our spirits soar,
Embracing paths we can explore.

In melodies of love's embrace,
We find our way, our perfect place.
The dance of life, a changing tune,
In second chances, we're immune.

So let us flow with every chance,
In laughter's light, we find our dance.
With open arms, we'll rise, we'll dare,
In every beat, there's love to share.

Beneath the Blossoms of Tomorrow

In quiet fields where dreams unfold,
Beneath the trees, tales to be told.
A whisper shared, a secret kept,
In gentle hearts, love's promise slept.

With petals soft, we venture near,
In every color, truths appear.
The light of dawn brings hope anew,
In every bloom, our love breaks through.

Through seasons change, we'll stand as one,
In life's embrace, our journey's begun.
The roots go deep, the branches wide,
In nature's grace, we will abide.

With every breeze, we'll sway and dance,
In blooming life, we seize our chance.
Beneath the stars, our dreams ignite,
In blossomed paths, we find our light.

So here we stand, as futures call,
In love's pure light, we'll never fall.
With open hearts and hands held high,
Beneath tomorrow's endless sky.

The Return of Sunlit Smiles

In morning light, we find our way,
The golden rays keep shadows at bay.
With laughter bright, we greet the day,
A joyous tune, come what may.

The soft breeze whispers secrets near,
While every heart beats loud and clear.
We chase our dreams, we hold them dear,
With sunlit smiles, we conquer fear.

Among the flowers, colors bloom,
Each vibrant shade dispels the gloom.
In every petal, joy has room,
Together, let our spirits zoom.

The world awakens, hope renewed,
With every hug, love's strength accrued.
In tender moments, hearts imbued,
With sunlit smiles, we are renewed.

So hand in hand, through days we steer,
With every laugh, we persevere.
In sunlight's glow, our path is clear,
The return of joy is finally here.

Cycles of Affection and Grace

Through seasons turn, our love will grow,
In every touch, we let it show.
With gentle words, like rivers flow,
In cycles of affection, we glow.

The moon will rise and then will wane,
Yet still we stand, through joy and pain.
In every loss, in every gain,
Our hearts remain, forever sane.

In twilight hours, we share our dreams,
With whispered hopes and silent screams.
Together forged, like flowing streams,
In cycles of love, or so it seems.

Through autumn leaves and winter's chill,
Our bond grows strong, we share the thrill.
With every moment, time stands still,
In cycles of affection, we will.

Through laughter loud and silence deep,
In memories made, our hearts we keep.
In gentle nights, when shadows creep,
In cycles of grace, love runs steep.

Heartbeats Reimagined

Each heartbeat sings a brand-new tune,
In quiet nights, beneath the moon.
With every pulse, our dreams are strewn,
In harmony, we find our boon.

The rhythm flows, a dance so sweet,
With every step, our spirits meet.
In every glance, our souls compete,
In heartbeats reimagined, we greet.

With every whisper, secrets share,
In moments still, we breathe the air.
Together we rise, beyond compare,
In love's embrace, nothing but fair.

Through trials faced and battles won,
As stars align, we become one.
In laughter bright, our fears are shun,
In heartbeats true, our journey's done.

So let us dream, our visions wide,
With every heartbeat, love our guide.
In every pulse, let's turn the tide,
In heartbeats reimagined, abide.

A Season of Us

In spring's embrace, new life appears,
Each bloom a promise, drying tears.
With every laugh, we conquer fears,
In this season of us, love nears.

Through summer days, our passion shines,
With sun-kissed skin and tangled vines.
With deepened hearts, it intertwines,
In warm caress, eternity aligns.

As autumn leaves begin to fall,
We'll hold each other through it all.
With golden hues, we hear love's call,
In this season of us, we stand tall.

In winter's chill, we find our heat,
With cozy nights, our hearts entreat.
Each icy breath, a rhythmic beat,
In this season of us, love's complete.

So raise a glass to moments shared,
In every season, hearts declared.
With time as witness, love bared,
A season of us, forever paired.

Stars Realigned in Our Universe

In the night sky, whispers call,
Guiding us through shadows small.
Galaxies twirl in a cosmic dance,
Our hearts aligned, a timeless chance.

Celestial bodies, bright and bold,
Stories of love and dreams unfold.
Radiant trails that light the way,
Together we'll journey, come what may.

Constellations sing, secrets shared,
In the vastness, our souls are bared.
Every spark a spark of grace,
In this universe, we find our place.

Bound by stardust, fate entwined,
A silent promise, hearts aligned.
Across the cosmos, we'll forever roam,
In the night sky, we have found home.

Through the dark, our path will blaze,
Guided by love in endless praise.
Stars once distant now shine on us,
In our universe, we'll always trust.

Reviving the Language of Touch

Fingers dance on skin so warm,
A silent vow, our hearts transform.
In every linger, love's embrace,
We find the words in a sacred space.

Whispers soft as evening's sigh,
A tender glance, a longing eye.
The pulse of love in every trace,
In this moment, we find our place.

Laughter interwoven with our bliss,
Every heartbeat feels like a kiss.
Bodies speaking, without a sound,
In the quiet, our truth is found.

We close the distance, let fears dissolve,
In the embrace where mysteries evolve.
The magic lives in gentle caress,
In the language of touch, we are blessed.

Reviving bonds that time forgot,
In each encounter, our spirits caught.
Together we dwell, a love's phoenix,
In every moment, our souls mix.

The Phoenix of Our Affection

From ashes dry, we rise anew,
With flames of passion, bright and true.
In the heart's furnace, love ignites,
Transforming shadows into lights.

We soared through storms, faced the night,
Together we found our inner light.
As embers glow, so fierce and bold,
A tale of love that must be told.

Wings spread wide, over valleys vast,
We leave behind what couldn't last.
In every trial, our strength we find,
A phoenix born, our souls entwined.

Through the fire, we shed our pain,
Emerging whole, we break the chain.
With every heartbeat, we affirm,
In love's embrace, we brightly burn.

Together we rise, no end in sight,
In the warmth of love's endless flight.
Soaring higher, we'll never tire,
In the phoenix of affection, we inspire.

A Tapestry of New Memories

Threads of laughter, woven tight,
In each moment, pure delight.
Patterns form in vibrant hues,
Every memory a love-infused muse.

Soft whispers echo in the night,
As stars bear witness to our light.
New stories bloom, like flowers bright,
A tapestry that feels so right.

Colors blend in a dance divine,
Every heartbeat writes a line.
Moments captured, never lost,
In this journey, love's the cost.

Through life's fabric, hand in hand,
We build a world, together we stand.
In every thread, a tale we weave,
In our hearts, we truly believe.

As seasons change, new memories grow,
In our tapestry, the love will flow.
Together we'll cherish, come what may,
In this woven dream, forever stay.

The Woven Path

In shadows cast by ancient trees,
We wander where the whispers tease.
With every step a tale unfolds,
A journey bright with dreams of gold.

The road unwinds like threads of fate,
Each moment sealed, each turn innate.
Through valleys deep and hills we climb,
We find our rhythm, dance with time.

Beneath the stars, our secrets hum,
A symphony of hearts that drum.
Together bound, we navigate,
This woven path that we create.

A Promise Reinvigorated

In the silence where we stand,
A promise made, a hopeful hand.
With every breath, we breathe anew,
The love that binds us, pure and true.

Time may falter, storms may rage,
Yet we shall turn another page.
With faith as strong as morning light,
We'll chase the shadows from our sight.

Through trials fierce, we learn to fight,
With courage bright, we claim our right.
To embrace the dawn, together rise,
A promise forged beneath the skies.

Ode to Our Resilience

In the face of every storm,
We find our strength, we transform.
Like rivers carve the ancient stone,
Our spirits soar, no longer lone.

With scars that tell our stories bold,
We cherish all the truths we hold.
Each stumble makes our roots run deep,
In unity, our dreams we keep.

Through darkest nights and trials fierce,
Our laughter shines, our hearts it pierce.
For in the struggle, we unite,
An ode to resilience, our light.

Unveiling the Heart

Behind the veil where secrets hide,
A world awaits, our hearts the guide.
With whispered truths and tender grace,
We unveil love's enchanting face.

Each layer peeled, a new delight,
The warmth of passion, pure and bright.
In vulnerability, we find,
A bond unbreakable, intertwined.

With every moment, stories grow,
Of laughter shared and tears that flow.
In the unveiling, we are free,
Embracing what we're meant to be.

Milton Keynes UK
Ingram Content Group UK Ltd.
UKHW021915281024
450365UK00017B/802